RUFFIAN

BY
DOROTHY CALLAHAN

To all who remember, and still shed a tear.

EDITED BY
DR. HOWARD SCHROEDER
**Professor In Reading and Language Arts
Dept. of Elementary Education
Mankato State University**

DESIGNED & PRODUCED BY
BAKER STREET PRODUCTIONS
MANKATO, MINNESOTA

**COVER GRAPHICS BY
BOB WILLIAMS**

CRESTWOOD HOUSE
Mankato, Minnesota

CIP

LIBRARY OF CONGRESS CATALOGING IN PUBLICATION DATA
Callahan, Dorothy M.
  Ruffian.

  (Horses, pasture to paddock)
  SUMMARY: Presents the life of a race horse whose successful career was
tragically cut short.
  1. Ruffian (Race Horse)--Biography--Juvenile literature. 2. Race horses--Bio-
graphy--Juvenile literature. 3. Horses--Biography--Juvenile literature. [1. Ruffian
(Race Horse). 2. Race horses. 3. Horses.] I. Schroeder, Howard. II. Baker Street
Productions. III. Title. IV. Series.
SF355.R8C34   1983   636.1'32   83-14382
ISBN 0-89686-231-3

International Standard Book Numbers:	Library of Congress Catalog Card Number:
Library Binding 0-89686-231-3	83-14382

PHOTOGRAPH CREDITS

Focus on Sports: Cover, 4, 24, 33, 45
Wide World: 6, 7, 29, 39, 41
New York Racing Association: 9, 14, 19, 34
Bob Coglianese/N.Y.R.A.: 30
Joseph DeMaria/N.Y.R.A.: 36
United Press International: 42

CRESTWOOD HOUSE

Hwy. 66 South, Box 3427
Mankato, MN 56002-3427

TABLE
OF
CONTENTS

As usually happened, Ruffian leads the field.

THE LOOK OF EAGLES: AN INTRODUCTION

She was an ebony phantom, whom no horse could defeat.

Her speed outpaced the cougar. Her grace outdanced the gazelle.

In the long history of horse racing, she was to be only a moment's magic. But she had "the look of eagles," which no man could forget.

① HIGH HOPES

Ruffian was born April 17, 1972, at Claiborne Farm in the bluegrass state of Kentucky.

From the moment her owners, the Stuart Janneys of Maryland, saw her, they knew she was special.

Her coat was a dark brown, baby-soft velvet that was almost black. She was the image of her grandfather, Bold Ruler, who had also lived at Claiborne. She even had a white star on her forehead.

Bold Ruler had been a championship runner and Horse of the Year in 1957. His sons, daughters, and grandchildren had won seventy-five big races all over the country. Six had been champion two-year-olds. Horsemen were calling him the greatest sire, or father horse, that ever lived.

Ruffian's grandfather, Bold Ruler, was known as the greatest sire that ever lived.

Ruffian's other grandfather was Native Dancer. Called "the great gray ghost," he had been Horse of the Year in 1952 and 1954. In his whole career, he had lost only one race — he was beaten by a neck in the 1953 Kentucky Derby.

Native Dancer's gray daughter, Shenanigans, was the little foal's mother. Reviewer was her father. He had won nine out of thirteen races.

With so many famous horses in her family, it was no wonder the Janneys had high hopes for the little one.

Ruffian had no trouble outrunning the other little fillies, or female horses, in her field at Claiborne. She

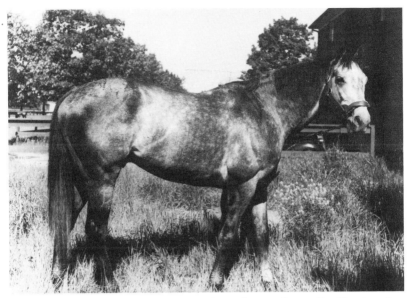

Native Dancer, called the "Great Gray Ghost," was Ruffian's other grandfather.

even held her own, running side by side with the colts, or male horses, in the next field.

Ruffian's tomboy name was just an accident. The Janneys had already sent an application for the name "Ruffian" to the Jockey Club, which keeps horse records. The Janneys meant to give the name to a colt they owned. But by the time the Jockey Club approved the name, the colt had been sold. Since the name had been accepted, they decided to give it to Shenanigans' strong little filly.

Ruffian's gentle nature and good manners always made the name sound wrong. But the first time she came out of a starting gate, it began to sound just right.

When Ruffian was nearly two years old, a special man came into her life.

Frank Whiteley, Jr. had been training horses for forty years. His stable had held many great ones. He was not easily impressed by good looks. He knew that in a racehorse, it was the part you didn't see that mattered — courage and the will to win.

Mr. Whiteley had come to Claiborne Farm in October of 1972, to look over the yearlings he would begin to train in the spring.

When he saw Ruffian, his face lit up just a bit. He ran his hands along her smooth, well-muscled body. He felt her forelegs and looked into her bluish-brown, deep-set eyes.

"She's one grand looking filly," he said. "But can she run?" Ruffian would show him.

②
A FILLY-IN-TRAINING

All thoroughbred horses change their official age on January 1. This keeps them in groups to compete against each other.

In January, 1974, Ruffian became a two-year-old. She was sent by van to the racehorse training center in Camden, South Carolina.

A young horse's legs are still growing and delicate at two years. If they run too hard on a track, they can be seriously injured. So Ruffian was just "ponied" around the soft dirt oval for a while. A man on another horse held tightly to her lead line and let her trot alongside him. She tugged and pulled to run faster, but he kept her back.

Once her legs had adjusted to the track surface, she got her first rider, John "Squeaky" Truesdale. He took her out for long, slow gallops of a mile or two. When Frank Whiteley thought she was ready, they began to breeze, or run fast for a short distance.

A racetrack is measured in furlongs, eight furlongs to a mile. In the beginning, Ruffian's breezes were only two furlongs in length, or a quarter of a

John "Squeaky" Truesdale was Ruffian's first rider.

9

mile. As she built up strength and stamina, her distances were increased.

All that winter, Ruffian worked out on the track. Each morning Frank arrived at the stable before dawn. He checked to see if her 4:30 breakfast had been eaten. A trainer knows a healthy horse is a hungry one.

Then he rode out to the track with Squeaky and watched Ruffian run. His stopwatch ticked off the seconds as she moved gracefully past each furlong pole.

"How's she moving?" Squeaky asked him one morning, after taking a slow lap around the track to let Ruffian calm down.

"She's moving!" Frank answered with a sly grin. Then he headed back to the barn.

Squeaky smiled to himself. He should have known better than to ask Mr. Whiteley about time. A good trainer didn't put all his faith in it. You had to see a horse run against another one before you knew if you had a winner.

Back at the barn, Ruffian was met by her groom and constant companion, Dan Williams. A trainer trusts his best horse only to his best groom. So Ruffian and Dan were a natural combination.

Dan unsaddled Ruffian and hosed down her body and legs. Then he tossed on her back, an old blue and yellow cooler, or horse blanket. Mr. Whiteley had won the blanket during his earlier days as a trainer.

10

It said "Charles Town" and had a half moon and stars, a symbol of night racing.

Dan led Ruffian around the stable area, walking her until he was sure she was cooled down. Her heart rate and breathing had to return to normal. Sometimes this took half an hour.

While he waited and watched, Frank studied Ruffian. The partnership between trainer and horse is made much easier if the trainer understands the animal's learning style and habits or personality. His horses' legs were always one of Frank's first concerns. So he never stopped watching Ruffian's.

Each morning when Ruffian felt the soft track beneath her feet, she leaped forward. She danced down the straightaway with grace and balance, on ankles no thicker than a man's wrist. She had a way of bobbing her head and running off sideways with a gentle, rocking motion. It was as though the whole jog was done to music only she could hear.

Even in the barn area, she moved with such smoothness, people turned to watch. She seemed to be "placing" each hoof, rather than landing on it.

Frank watched her nearly every day, but still he had trouble reading her thoughts. No bird or flying piece of paper escaped her eye. Her ears pricked and turned in the direction of each sound. All the while she had a faraway look that seemed to carry her beyond man's limited vision.

"You know, Dan," Frank said to his groom one

morning. "She has it — that look of eagles in her eye."

"Yes sir. I been noticing it myself. Kind of like she sees something out there that we can't see."

"Only the great ones have it," Frank continued. "They would rather die than let anything get by them on the track. Breaks their hearts to lose."

Frank quickly stood up and folded his chair. He had begun to dream and he had to shake himself out of it. When a trainer had a promising runner, he had to keep reminding himself it was only an animal. But with this magnificent animal, dreaming was easy.

"Well, we'll soon find out how great she is, Dan," Frank added. "It's time we packed up and went to the races in New York."

③
OFF TO NEW YORK

In the spring, the whole Whiteley stable of horses moved North.

Belmont Park is a racetrack on Long Island about twenty miles from New York City. It is run by the New York Racing Association. Some of the finest horses in the world compete there. The barn area is green and country-like. But it is surrounded by houses, traffic and people.

By the beginning of May, Ruffian had adjusted to

life on the Belmont "backstretch." She had been working with other horses in the starting gate. They learned to stand quietly when the doors were closed behind them. The horses sprang forward with a rush when the front doors opened.

Early each morning Yates Kennedy, Ruffian's other exercise rider, took her out on the track. She usually galloped with another horse from her stable. They ran more for exercise than speed.

Then one day Frank sent her out with a filly from his son David's stable. The other filly was ridden by an exercise girl.

Together the pair jogged along, loosening up. Both riders had been told to let their horses run when they reached the three-eighths pole.

Frank leaned against the rail in front of the stands as both horses came to the stretch, or final turn. When they passed the candy-striped pole that marked three furlongs to go, the riders urged their horses on.

Ruffian took the lead. But Yates kept a tight hold on her, training her to save speed for a final burst.

As they began running the last quarter-mile to the finish line, the other horse pulled alongside. Ruffian saw it.

She pricked her ears, then pulled them back. She seemed to feel a challenge to her right to be in front. Digging her hind hooves deeply into the sandy loam of the track, she lurched forward. Yates let her go.

She sped off, leaving the other horse far behind.

Yates was chuckling when the exercise girl caught up to them beyond the finish line.

"What's that you're riding, greased lightning?" she asked.

Back at the rail, Frank was not chuckling. He was staring at his stopwatch.

"What was that all about?" he asked Yates.

"She must have thought that the other filly wanted to pass her," Yates answered. "She just took off."

"That's the last time she breezes in company," Frank said. "She'll burn herself out working that fast."

In a booth high above the finish line, the official clockers had their stopwatches out, too. They

Trainer Frank Whiteley watches Ruffian work out.

14

nodded their heads as they wrote down Ruffian's time for three furlongs.

But like Frank Whiteley, they had seen too many "morning glories." These were horses that bloomed like winners in the workouts, but faded in the afternoon race.

"She's got speed," they said. "But let's wait and see."

④
MAIDEN RACE

Frank Whiteley knew the time was right for Ruffian's first race. She seemed nervous. Frank knew some horses got edgy and bored standing in their twelve foot by twelve foot stall twenty-four hours a day. So he had Dan take Ruffian out for a walk each afternoon to nibble grass in the barn area. Then Dan hosed down her legs to keep them relaxed.

But Ruffian's energy could not be contained. She began nipping playfully at the stablehands. Even Dan got a nudge or nibble if he wasn't careful.

The Condition Book for May was issued by Belmont's Racing Secretary. It was the Secretary's job to put together races for all the horses stabled at Belmont. They were then published in a booklet which listed the conditions for each race.

Frank found the perfect one for Ruffian. It was a

maiden race, a competition for horses which have never won before.

Next Frank had to find the right jockey for his strong, eager filly. He often used Jacinto Vasquez as his rider. Jacinto had been coming around the stable lately, hoping to get Ruffian for a mount.

This hard-riding Panamanian was one of the ten top jockeys in the United States. Frank was looking for a rider who wanted to win as much as Ruffian seemed to. But it had to be somebody who could control her great speed and strength until the end of the race.

Frank let Jacinto take her out in the morning and work her from the starting gate. They broke away from the gate quickly and Jacinto let Ruffian run for a quarter of a mile. Then he tried to slow her down. Still she ran. With all his strength he tightened the reins until she felt his signal.

Frank was laughing when they rode over to him. "Well, what do you think?" he asked.

"I never rode a horse like this," Jacinto said excitedly. "She knows what she's doing. She wants to run and I want to ride her."

On the day of the maiden race, Ruffian sensed that something was different. Instead of her workout, Dan just walked her around the barn. When the time came for lunch, she had only a few oats. She whinnied and snorted, but Dan just took her outside the stall and painted her hoofs with hoof polish until they shone.

Then he buckled on her new leather bridle. It had a gold name tag that said RUFFIAN in large letters and had her parents names in small ones under it.

Dan walked her down the path that led to the paddock. This is a grassy area with stalls, where the horses for each race are saddled.

People were everywhere, trying to get a look at the horses before they ran. But Frank didn't let them look too long at Ruffian. He didn't want her to get nervous. So he saddled her up and told Jacinto to pass up the paddock parade and go straight to the track.

There were ten horses in the field. The Racing Secretary had held a drawing the previous day. Each horse's number and post position in the gate were picked in the drawing.

Ruffian had gotten number nine. This was not a good spot, because it was far to the outside. Since the track has an oval shape, the outside horse must cover more ground to get to an inside spot near the rail.

As the race was about to begin, the assistant starter took Ruffian's reins and led her into the starting gate. Jacinto braced himself for a quick take-off by holding onto Ruffian's mane.

Suddenly all the doors on the gate sprang open with a loud thump as the electrical current, which held them closed, was switched off.

For a moment Ruffian was left behind. Jacinto urged her forward. She eagerly charged at the leaders who were spread across the track. Before the first two furlong poles had been passed, Ruffian took the lead.

Jacinto could feel Ruffian's muscles extend beneath him. He tightened his grip and guided her in toward the rail. If he hadn't felt her hoofs hitting one at a time, he would have thought they were flying.

The crowd was shouting as they passed the grandstand and crossed the finish line. Jacinto looked back and saw that the nearest horse was fifteen horse-lengths behind them.

The jockey stood up in the stirrups to signal Ruffian that the race was over. She jogged along for another half mile, letting her muscles slowly relax.

When they met Frank in the winner's circle, the track announcer was saying, "It is now official. The winner, Ruffian, a dark brown filly by Reviewer out of Shenanigans. Equaling the track record of one minute, three seconds."

As Frank and Dan walked off the track with Ruffian, some reporters shouted toward them. "Hey, Frank. You got any more in your barn who can run like that?"

Frank took his eyes off Ruffian's legs for a moment. "If I did, it would scare me to death," he said.

⑤
FINISHING THE SEASON

The next day, the newspaper called Ruffian's victory, "The greatest race ever run by a first-time starter."

Now Ruffian was no longer a maiden racehorse. She was a winner.

Her next race at Belmont Park was the Fashion Stakes for two-year-old fillies. Once again she won, equaling the record for that stakes race.

On July 10, 1974, Ruffian went to nearby Aqueduct racetrack for the Astoria Stakes. With each

Ruffian is photographed in the winner's circle with jockey Jacinto Vasquez, after winning the Fashion Stakes.

added month, she grew bigger and stronger. Her racing ability improved and her competition grew slim. Trainers were not willing to have their horses risk such overwhelming defeat at her hands. She proved them right by winning the Astoria by nine lengths. She led the race from "wire to wire," or start to finish.

Ruffian was taken to Monmouth Park in New Jersey for the running of the Sorority Stakes on July 24, 1974. It promised to be her first real challenge. Hot 'N' Nasty, her main opponent, was also undefeated.

"Hey there. What's eating you today?" Dan Williams asked as he walked Ruffian to the paddock. She was pulling back on the lead shank and scanning the unfamiliar area with a fearful eye.

"What's got her so stirred up, Dan?" Frank asked as he saddled his horse.

"She's been jumpy since we got here, Mr. Whiteley," Dan replied. "Never been like this before."

Frank was uneasy, too, as he walked out front to watch the race.

Both Ruffian and her rival broke evenly out of the gate. Together they took off around the backstretch area, across from the grandstand. Ruffian ran along the rail and logged her fastest quarter-mile ever. But she still had only a half-length lead.

Ruffian edged forward. But as they rounded the stretch turn, Hot 'N' Nasty began to run harder.

Jacinto, bent low over Ruffian's neck, could hear her heavy breathing. He gripped her shoulders with his knees, his seat just above the saddle. By balancing his weight over Ruffian, the jockey could work his hands and body to her forward rhythm.

Hot 'N' Nasty kept inching up on the outside.

Like all jockeys, Jacinto carried a whip as part of his equipment. Some horses needed a few taps to get them going. Others just needed it waved at them and they took off.

Jacinto had never needed to touch Ruffian with it before. Now he could take no chances. He waved 'the stick' past her eyes. Then he gave her one sharp tap on the rump.

The result was like pushing the gas pedal of a car to the floor. Ruffian spurted off to win by two and a quarter lengths. Jacinto never had to use the whip on her again.

Each summer in August the New York Racing Association season moves upstate to Saratoga, New York. Saratoga has the oldest working track in the United States. It is the home of the National Museum of Racing. Its clean air and country atmosphere give everyone on the race circuit a vacation feeling.

Saratoga has been called "the graveyard of champions" because famous horses such as Man o' War and Secretariat have been defeated there. But it is also called "the cradle of champions." Many two-year-olds, who go on to greatness, first show their ability here during its late summer meetings.

The Spinaway Stakes at Saratoga matches horses who are hopeful of winning the Triple Crown series for fillies the following year. The three races for the Triple Crown Series are the Acorn, the Mother Goose, and the Coaching Club American Oaks.

If a filly were good enough she could enter the big Triple Crown series open to any three-year-old: The Kentucky Derby, The Preakness and the Belmont Stakes.

People thought Ruffian was good enough to enter the big Triple Crown. Only one filly before had ever won the Derby race, which is the first race for the Triple Crown. In fifteen years, none had even tried.

In the back of his mind Frank thought Ruffian was good enough, too. But he wouldn't discuss it. "I take one race at a time," he told reporters. With the risk a horse took each time it stepped on a track, he felt it was the only way to think.

At Spinaway Stakes post time Ruffian was the stand-out favorite of the crowd. Frank boosted jockey Vince Bracciale into the saddle. Jacinto was under suspension for a riding violation he had committed a few days before.

Ruffian seemed not to notice the jockey change. She pranced onto the track, bowing her neck and sidestepping toward the rail as cameras clicked. Her ebony black coat glistened in the summer sunshine.

"They're off," the announcer shouted as the horses left the gate at the six-furlong pole. Ruffian quickly took the lead. As she drew near the stands at the finish line she increased her lead.

Ruffian was ahead by thirteen lengths when the electric timer on the infield board stopped. She had run the fastest three-quarters of a mile in Saratoga's one-hundred-seven-year history.

Twelve seconds for every furlong is considered good running time in races which are a mile or less. Ruffian's time of sixty-nine seconds cut three big seconds off the average time. In a sport where time is measured in fifths of a second, that was an eternity.

Ruffian had defeated the best fillies in her age group. They were fighting each other to stay in her shadow. Yet she had made them look as though they were out for a Sunday stroll. There were a few more races she could enter this fall to increase her earnings. Then it would be back to South Carolina for a winter rest.

⑥
THE BUBBLE BURSTS

Trainers are worriers by nature. When things go well for a long time, they don't relax and enjoy it. They worry even more that the good bubble will burst.

Dan Williams leads Ruffian onto the track at the start of a race.

Each time Ruffian won, Frank tried to fight the rumor that she was unbeatable. "She's a lovely filly," he would say. "She's got speed and class. But I can't have her perfect for every race. They all get beaten someday."

Ruffian had won $134,000. Her next race was to be the Frizette Stakes on September 24th for a purse, or prize money, of $100,000.

The Janneys had come from Maryland especially to see her run.

Early that morning Frank came to the stable as usual. But he found something unusual. Ruffian had not eaten her breakfast. Her eyes lacked sparkle and her body felt warm.

The thermometer read one degree above normal as Frank held it up to the light. "That does it, Dan," he said. "Get the Doc. She won't race today unless she's completely well."

The crowd at the track groaned in disappointment as the announcer told them that Ruffian would be scratched, or withdrawn.

The next morning Ruffian's feed bucket was empty and she was looking for more.

"Full of vinegar this morning, Mr. Whiteley," Dan said. He clipped a lead shank on her halter and led her out of the stall.

"Wait a minute. What was that?" Frank asked as Ruffian walked past him. "I thought I just saw her limp a little."

Though he did not see it again, Frank told Dan, "Just walk her for a few days. No workouts. Hose those legs down and cool them off in case she's sore."

Frank continued to spend every extra minute

watching Ruffian's legs. Toward the end of the week, he saw her misstep again. He went straight to the phone and called his veterinarian, Jim Prendergast.

"Better get right over and bring your X-ray machine," he said.

Dr. Prendergast took many X rays of Ruffian's hind quarters. Carefully, he studied them. The major bones were all whole, no chips. The sesamoids, two small knoblike bones at the back of the ankle joint were intact.

Back at his office, the doctor checked the X rays again. He saw a fine line shadow in the pastern bone, just above the hoof of the right hind leg.

"It's just a hairline fracture," he told Frank. "But I'm afraid it will keep her off the track for the rest of the year."

Frank couldn't help feeling unhappy. For the first time in his life, he had begun to plan beyond the next race. It had backfired on him.

Ruffian would surely win top honors as the 1974, two-year-old filly of the year. No one else could come near. One or two more victories might even have made her the overall Horse of the Year.

But there was no use thinking about what might have been. Ruffian had to be repaired first.

"We'll have to put a cast on the lower part of her leg for about six weeks," Dr. Prendergast said. "She may not like it."

Frank knew that the hardest part of treating an

injured horse was getting it to accept the treatment. He had seen horses fight the medicine or operation that could keep them alive. Often a high-spirited thoroughbred would refuse to keep a cast on.

Dan and Frank talked softly to Ruffian and stroked her as the veterinarian fixed the lightweight, fiberglass cast in place. She seemed calm.

Back in her stall, Ruffian decided to fight the stiff restraint. She began pounding her right hind leg against the boards.

"Whoa, girl. Whoa," Dan hollered. Then he ran to the phone. "Better get back over here fast, Doc," he said. "She's trying to kick the cast off."

Dr. Prendergast shook his head. "Our only hope is a pillow cast," he said. "She might think it's part of her regular bandages."

"We've got to try it, Doc," Frank said, the worry apparent in his voice. "We've got no other choice."

The vet began winding layers of cotton bandage tightly around Ruffian's leg. It was like the elastic binding human athletes wear. Then Dan put her regular stall bandages on the other legs. These were used on all horses to keep them from getting bumps and scratches in their stalls.

This time Ruffian accepted the treatment.

By November her X rays showed perfect healing. So Frank took her to the milder climate of Camden, South Carolina, to get back into condition. He had decided not to run her against the boys in the Kentucky Derby. He would not risk another injury. Ruffian would shoot for the filly Triple Crown. If she bounced back well from the fracture, she should win the crown.

⑦
BACK ON THE TRACK

On April 14, 1975, Ruffian ran in an allowance race at Aqueduct. It was a contest run for horses of lesser ability. Frank wanted to see if she was ready to step back into stakes, or major race, competition.

She had to carry more weight than the other horses, because she had a much better winning record.

Ruffian seemed a bit nervous when she came onto the track. Jacinto Vasquez, her jockey, whispered some soothing words into her ear and let her run off to loosen up her muscles. She had been away from racing for ten months. Some of the sounds had become strange again.

But as soon as the gate opened, her natural response returned. She knew only one way to run — get out in front and stay there.

As Frank led Ruffian from the winner's circle, he was happy. Trainers fear that a long winter layover can take the winning edge off a horse. It hadn't bothered Ruffian a bit.

The Comely Stakes, which is seven furlongs in length, was run on April 30, 1975. Ruffian had her head down and left the gate last. Jacinto rushed her forward. She took the lead and never gave it up. Arriving at the finish line eight lengths in front, she set a race record. It was the fastest Comely ever run.

Ruffian was ready for the filly Triple Crown. She had never looked sharper. Frank wasn't worried about the longer distance of each race. Jacinto usually spent half the distance around the track, holding her back.

In the mile-long Acorn Stakes at Aqueduct on May 10, 1975, she took off first and stayed there.

Ruffian wins easily at Aqueduct.

Ruffian floated home like a feather on her own breeze, a winner by eight lengths. Again she set a new record for the race.

The newspapers compared her effortless speed to that of Foolish Pleasure. This colt who also had Bold Ruler for a grandfather, had won the Kentucky Derby a week before. Ruffian was faster at a mile distance than he was.

But the Derby had been run at a mile and an eighth. Three weeks later, Ruffian won the Mother Goose Stakes at that distance a full second faster than Foolish Pleasure's Derby time. It seemed to everyone who took their stopwatches seriously, that Ruffian could have won the Derby with ease.

Ruffian is shown with her owner, Stuart Janney.

Frank Whiteley noticed the two sets of times, too. He wondered if he had made a mistake in not running her against the colts in the Kentucky Derby.

But it was too late now. The last leg of the filly Triple Crown, the Coaching Club American Oaks, was coming up in a few weeks.

The reporters gave him no rest. "When, when, when . . ." they kept asking Frank. Ruffian against the boys. It had to be, or how could she be called the Horse of the Year for 1975?

The New York Racing Association was working on a Race of Champions. It would bring together the three different horses which had won a part of the big Triple Crown series — Foolish Pleasure had won the Derby; Master Derby, the Preakness; and Avatar, the Belmont Stakes.

Ruffian's name was not mentioned. Frank felt this was the race where she belonged if there had to be a showdown.

Then a new idea surfaced. Foolish Pleasure's trainer LeRoy Jolley said that he would be willing to race his horse against Ruffian, but only on a one-to-one basis. That way each horse knew the one it had to beat and the trainers could plan a way to do it.

The idea of a match race did not appeal to Frank. He knew the dangers of injury when two horses were locked in a blazing head-to-head battle. But when Ruffian's owners agreed, he accepted the challenge.

The sports pages came alive with the news. Suddenly horse racing shared top headlines with baseball. There hadn't been a match race in New York in twenty-eight years. The last male-female match had taken place in Mexico in 1914.

But this was 1975. Women were fighting for "equal rights" with men in careers and sports. Somehow this competition between Ruffian and Foolish Pleasure took on a stature bigger than a horse race. It became a "battle of the sexes."

Buttons marked HER sprang up on women's lapels all over the city. Others marked HIM were worn by men. It was all good-natured fun.

The details of the race were published. It would be a mile-and-a-quarter contest held at Belmont Park on July 6, 1975. The winner would receive a purse of $225,000. The loser would get $125,000 just for finishing.

Foolish Pleasure would have a month to train for the race. But Ruffian still had the Oaks ahead. It was her first test at a mile and a half. Foolish Pleasure had clocked an excellent time at that distance, of 2:28 1/5 when he lost by a nose in the Belmont Stakes. Frank hoped Ruffian could do better.

Everyone knew if she were beaten in this last leg of the filly Triple Crown, the match race would not be so important.

Thirty thousand people were on hand for the Coaching Club Oaks, the final race of the filly Triple Crown. Ruffian left the gate with long, loping strides and took the lead. Jacinto felt comfortable, until he heard the crowd screaming and looked over his shoulder.

Braulio Baeza, the jockey who was to ride Foolish Pleasure in the match race, was closing in on them. His horse Equal Change was gaining.

Ruffian seemed to sense the danger, too. She stretched her stride and pulled off majestically to win by three lengths.

The people cheered with delight. Now the match race would really be a contest. Ruffian's time was faster than Foolish Pleasure's, but only by two-fifths of a second.

Frank squeezed his way to the winner's circle. He

Ruffian is off to another fast start.

By winning the Coaching Club Oaks, Ruffian won the filly Triple Crown.

checked Ruffian's legs. Then he looked into those faraway eyes. He knew she was a "Superfilly," as everyone said. But he was not one to brag. She had won all ten of her races in blistering time, equaling or beating a record in nine of them. He would let the reporters write their battles with words. He had a horse to train.

⑧
THE SHOWDOWN

Training for the match race meant training for speed and endurance. Frank knew LeRoy Jolley would have one plan for beating Ruffian. She had never been pressed and never passed. Foolish Pleasure would come out of the gate trying to do both. Frank hoped there would be a chance for the horses to relax and slow their pace. But he wasn't counting on it.

Ruffian turned in some blazing workouts. One morning she covered five furlongs in fifty-eight seconds. Two days later, Foolish Pleasure went the distance in fifty-seven.

Some horsemen began to worry. When the times were that low, it could mean the track was too fast and too dry. That was hard on a horse's legs.

A special chute was built at the backstretch corner of the track. It would allow the horses to run in a

"Squeaky" wears a special Ruffian T-shirt.

straight line for three-quarters of a mile. They would not have to make the turn that a mile and a quarter race usually required.

Reporters and photographers from around the world planned to be at the race. CBS television would send the picture to a million viewers.

When Squeaky Truesdale, Ruffian's exercise rider, took her out for a morning breeze, he wore a red and white Ruffian T-shirt like her many other fans.

Track veterinarian Manuel Gilman had both horses "weigh-in" like prize fighters. Ruffian brought her usual calm manner to the scale. But

Foolish Pleasure kicked as though he were angry to be shorter and sixty-four pounds lighter. Only his feet were larger. So he would be able to absorb the impact of his lighter weight on a wider surface than she.

July 6th finally arrived. Fifty thousand fans filled the racetrack on a day that grew dark and ominous as the afternoon wore on. Thunder and lightning cracked in the distance. People took cover and hoped the weather would clear by the day's feature race, the eighth race on the program.

By six o'clock the skies had brightened. The fun-filled atmosphere returned to the crowd. Last minute teasing about the "weaker sex" continued.

Even horsemen in the clubhouse section had pushed the danger of match racing from their mind. They had flown in from all over the world and were ready to enjoy the contest.

Everyone came to their feet as the horses trotted onto the track. Number one, Ruffian, was a slight favorite to win. Her coat gleamed like black satin, as she gently jogged off down the track. Jacinto stood in the stirrups, wearing the red and white silks of Janney's Locust Hill Farm.

The jockey had made a hard choice in riding her in this race. He was also Foolish Pleasure's regular rider. Together they had won the Derby.

Jacinto felt a stronger loyalty to Frank and Ruffian though, so he chose to ride the filly. But he knew

Foolish Pleasure was a courageous colt and that Braulio Baeza was a skillful jockey. They would be a tough combination to beat.

As both horses trotted past the winner's circle, their reflection flashed in the two hundred-year-old silver trophy that would go to the winner. In 1804, this trophy had been won by a woman who rode her filly to victory over one of the best male jockeys of the day.

Frank focused his binoculars on Ruffian as the horses neared the chute. Like a queen, she bobbed her head to the backstretch crew that had lined the rail to pay her homage.

The loudspeaker crackled. "It is now post time." Frank drew a deep breath. Down at trackside, Dan's hands tightly clutched Ruffian's empty lead shank. "You've gotta show that colt," he whispered. "Now go!"

The bell sounded. "And they're off," said the announcer. "Breaking sharply, Foolish Pleasure on the outside puts a head in front."

Driving forward Ruffian gained her usual edge. She was up front, trying to pull ahead. But Foolish Pleasure stayed alongside. The jockeys crouched low over their horses' necks. They were riding as though the finish line were just ahead, not a whole mile to go.

"Ruffian is in the lead by a nose," the announcer said. "The first quarter-mile in twenty-two and one-fifth seconds, a very fast pace for a long race."

As the horses crossed from the softer dirt of the chute to the drier surface of the main track, Foolish Pleasure made a move.

Jacinto had hoped to slow the pace and save Ruffian's speed for the end of the race. But the colt kept pushing, so she had to keep up.

As her opponent edged forward, Ruffian changed her stride. She extended her forelegs and dug her hind legs in deeply.

The dim noise of the crowd seemed miles away on the other side of the track. The jockeys were only aware of the thud of hoofbeats and the puffing of their horses' deep breathing.

Suddenly a sickening snap pierced the air. Both jockeys heard it. But only Jacinto felt it. Ruffian had

Ruffian starts to fall behind Foolish Pleasure, after breaking her ankle on the backstretch of Belmont Park.

broken a bone in her right ankle, but she kept on running.

Jacinto used all his strength to try pulling her up. But her mind and body held one desire — put a head in front, run hard, never be passed.

As she ran, she drove dirt into the wound that opened when there was no longer a strong ankle bone to support her leg. By the time Jacinto stopped her flight and jumped off, she had gone seventy more yards. She was bleeding badly. Her eyes rolled wildly in pain and shock. Her foreleg below the ankle was turned up like a ski tip.

At the first misstep, Frank knew what had happened and began to run across the infield.

Hollow cheers for the winner, Foolish Pleasure, echoed behind him. But most eyes were trained on the backstretch hedge where Ruffian limped helplessly.

Dr. Gilman arrived in the horse ambulance. Ruffian was even pulling away from Dan, her eyes glazed and unknowing.

"It doesn't look good, Frank," the veterinarian said. Then he wrapped a balloon-like pressure cast around Ruffian's leg and inflated it.

They managed to get her back to the barn. The best animal doctors in the world gathered at her stall.

Her heart rate could not be brought down in the usual cooling-out walk. So the doctors tried medica-

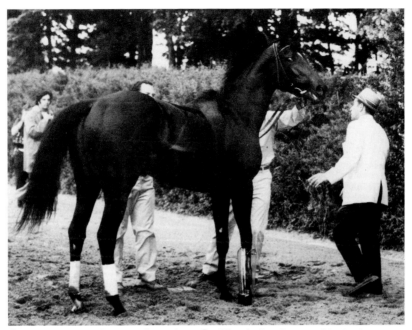

A pressure cast was placed on Ruffian's broken ankle before she was taken off the track.

tion. But Ruffian did not understand. Her body was lathered with sweat. In her mind she was still on the racetrack, running, trying to win.

Frank and Dan plunged her leg in ice water to try to stop the bleeding. But it continued.

An operation had to be done. Her racing career was over, but it could save her life. Dr. William Reed's Equine Hospital was across from the track. Ruffian was taken there. X rays showed that both Ruffian's sesamoid bones at the ankle joint had been shattered. She had continued to run on raw bone, pushing dirt into the wound.

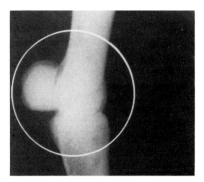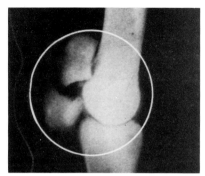

X rays of a normal ankle (left) and Ruffian's broken ankle (right).

Mr. Janney was told that there was only a one-in-ten chance of saving her. Everyone knew if it had been any other horse, it would have been "put down."

But this was Ruffian. A few minutes ago she had run her heart out for the crowd as they cheered for HER. Now all that was meaningless. All that mattered to anyone was the race for her life.

A medical doctor from New York Hospital, who designed casts for human injuries, was called. With the help of a blacksmith, he forged a special "shoe" for Ruffian. It had to take the weight off the severe injury. At the same time, it must allow her to stand while the damage healed.

Waiting outside the operating room, Dan and Frank did not have to speak. They both knew Ruffian's breeding was against her. She was born to run. It was all she wanted to do. Once before she had shown her dislike for a cast.

Yet they remembered she had come through that injury with a kind of royal patience. With racing fans across the country, they could only wait and hope.

After two hours of surgery, Ruffian was taken to the padded recovery room. The operation was a success and the special shoe was in place. Now everything depended on how the filly reacted when she awoke. If she accepted the cast and it bore her weight, there was a chance.

Ruffian's eyes blinked open. Her legs began to move as she lay on her side. The doctors came close, trying to comfort and encourage her.

She began to struggle. She tried to raise her head, but it fell back.

"Come on, girl. Take it easy," someone said. But she couldn't be calmed.

Her front legs began moving in a swimming motion. It was what the doctors feared most. Faster the legs churned, as though she were still racing from an unseen challenger.

Finally she pounded the wounded leg against the floor. The cast began to slip. Blood showed through the bandages.

Dr. Reed shook his head and left the room.. "It's no use," he told Frank and Mr. Janney. "We can't repeat the operation. The anesthesia would kill her."

"Don't let her suffer anymore. She's too great for that," they said. Ruffian was given a large dose of a tranquilizer. At last her anxious spirit was at rest.

⑨
HER SPIRIT LINGERS

Two hours later, Frank was back at the barn. "No horse will ever stand in this stall again," he told Dan. "No horse will be worthy."

As the stablehands drifted in, Frank pushed them to keep up their routine. Through their tears, they got the other horses out as usual.

That evening when the last racing fan had passed through the gate, a huge bulldozer began its work.

It rolled to a spot in front of the clubhouse stands and began to ready a gravesite for Ruffian.

The sun had set and twilight had fallen around the small band of Ruffian's family. The horse van pulled to a spot just beyond the finish line where she would lie, her race over at last.

Frank brought two blankets to cover her. One was the "royal robe" he got her when she was voted top filly. The other was the old blue and yellow cooler with the half moon and stars. She had worn it when she was special only to Dan and him.

The Racing Association flag flew at half-mast above her resting place. It mourned the passing of promises left unfulfilled.

But those who had seen Ruffian run would remember her as she had always been — undefeated and in the lead — even at the end.

She had the look of eagles.

GLOSSARY

BACKSTRETCH - Barn area; also, the area of the racetrack opposite the finish line and grandstand.

BREEZE - A fast workout for a short distance, run in order to time a horse.

CONDITION BOOK - Book issued by the Racing Secretary, which explains the rules and conditions for entering a horse in a particular race.

FILLY TRIPLE CROWN - Means victory in three races run in New York for female three-year-old horses: The Acorn, The Mother Goose and the Coaching Club American Oaks.

FURLONG - Measure of distance on a racetrack equal to one-eighth of a mile.

GALLOP - Slow workout, done for exercise.

HORSE OF THE YEAR - Eclipse Award winner, as most outstanding racehorse in a particular year, regardless of age or sex.

JOCKEY CLUB - Thoroughbred agency which approves horses' names and records their ancestry for the *American Stud Book*.

PADDOCK - Area on racetrack grounds where horses are saddled before a race.

PONYING - As part of its first training on a race-track, a young horse is "ponied" — allowed to try its legs on a track, trotting alongside a lead horse.

RACING SECRETARY - Person who designs races at the track to fit the horses that are stabled there.

SILKS - Shirt and cap cover usually made of nylon in the owner's colors.

STAKES RECORD - The fastest time recorded in the history of a particular race.

STAKES (SWEEPSTAKES) - A major horserace in which an owner must post an entry fee for his horse. The fees become part of the purse, or winnings, to be divided among the top finishers.

SUSPENSION - A period in which a jockey may not compete in the races. It is a penalty imposed by the judges for a violation of racing rules, such as interfering with another horse's chance to win a race.

TRACK RECORD - The fastest time recorded for a distance on a particular track.

TRIPLE CROWN - The term used to designate a victory in the Kentucky Derby, Preakness and Belmont Stakes, in which a three-year-old horse of either sex may compete.

THE HORSES

PASTURE TO PADDOCK

CRESTWOOD HOUSE